Endorsements

Sharon Norris Elliott has masterfully woven a tender tapestry of vulnerability, wisdom, and spiritual guidance in *After Him: A Widow's First Year Devotional Journal*. With the heart of a storyteller, the depth of a seasoned teacher, and the compassion of someone who has walked this path, Sharon offers a lifeline to those navigating the uncharted waters of loss. This book is more than a journal; it's a companion, providing a safe space for reflection, a roadmap for processing grief, and a gentle invitation to wrestle with God and find His blessings in the midst of pain. Whether you are a widow, a caregiver, or someone walking alongside a grieving friend, this devotional memoir will inspire and comfort you in profound ways. I wholeheartedly recommend it to anyone seeking solace, hope, and a deeper connection to God during life's most challenging seasons.

---Linda Evans Shepherd, author of *Praying Through Hard Times*

Healing is found within the pages of this new book, written by my dear friend, Dr. Sharon Elliott. Having been given an occasional window into her grieving process, this book comes from an authentic place of love, grace, and empathy—all from the heart of God. Sharon understands that although the person who has now passed can never be replaced, there is "Balm in Gilead." Be encouraged through the words in this book.

---Skot Welch, Author of *Unfractured: A Christ-Centered Action Plan for Cultural Change* and *Plantation Jesus: Race, Faith and a New Way Forward*

I wholeheartedly endorse *After Him: A Widow's First Year Devotional Journal* by Sharon Norris Elliott. This poignant and beautifully crafted book offers a raw and honest exploration of grief, resilience, and hope. Elliott's reflective journaling captures the profound emotions that accompany loss, making it a powerful companion for anyone navigating the complexities of widowhood.

Her writing is both intimate and relatable, inviting readers to join her on a journey through heartache and healing. With each entry,

she provides not only a glimpse into her personal experience but also practical insights and encouragement for others facing similar struggles.

After Him serves as a comforting reminder that while grief can feel isolating, shared experiences can foster connection and understanding. Elliott's ability to articulate the nuances of loss makes this book an invaluable resource for widows and their loved ones. It's a testament to the strength of the human spirit and a beautiful tribute to love that endures beyond death. I highly recommend this book to anyone seeking solace and guidance in their own journey of grief.

> ---Pastor Welton Pleasant II, Senior Pastor of
> Christ Second Baptist Church, Long Beach, CA

Compassionate, empathetic, down-to-earth, gently understanding: these are just a few words that describe Dr. Sharon Norris Elliott's new book *After Him: A Widow's First Year Devotional Journal*. Dr. Sharon walked through the valley of the shadow of death holding tightly to the Shepherd's hand, so she knows intimately of the Lord's tender ability to comfort a widow at this most difficult time. As a pastor, I often must be involved with the widow as she says goodbye to her husband, so I appreciate having this book to serve as another widow's compassionate voice that can say, "I know just how you feel." I highly recommend this book as it can become the anchor needed for widows in challenging times.

> ---Bishop Tom B. Watson, Senior Pastor of
> Watson Memorial Teaching Ministries, New Orleans, LA

After Him

A Widow's First Year Devotional Journal

By Dr. Sharon Norris Elliott

Abundance Books

After Him: A Widow's First Year Devotional Journal
Copyright © 2025 Dr. Sharon Norris Elliott

ISBN: 978-1-963377-36-1
Published by Abundance Books, LLC
abundance-books.com

10 9 8 7 6 5 4 3 2 1

Interior design by Taryn Golliher
Cover design by Jenn Dafoe-Turner

Dedication

This book is dedicated to all the strong, beautiful widows in my life.

Saundra Nelson, my sister

Esther Norris, my sister-in-love

Dawn Nelson, my niece

Lanette Black, my friend

and

All the widows at Christ Second Baptist Church, Long Beach, California. Especially those who consistently reach out to comfort me:

Betty Miller

Carolyn Chubbs

Ophelia Sanders

Ruby Richards

and

Mother Maggie Reid

You weather this unique brand of grief with incredible grace. You are shining examples of how to carry on while allowing God to carry you through each new day after your "him" moved to Paradise. You continue to be nourished by God's daily new mercies, and whether you have remarried or not, having traversed the "valley of the shadow of death," you've been imbued with a special, heavenly ability to continue to nourish us all with understanding, smiles, food, wisdom, and love.

Thank you.

Acknowledgements

Thank you to the Trinity for carrying me through this season of grief.

James D. Elliott, my late husband, you made this book possible by being such a strong Black man and such a force on the planet. You knew who you were, who you loved, and who you served as your Lord and Savior. I have to give you this posthumous gratitude. I still miss you.

Thank you to my pastor, Rev. Welton Pleasant II, and his wife, my friend, Teresa Pleasant. I don't know how you do it, but you are always there when I need you.

Jerod, Lori, Datton, and Chad, James's children, thank you for all you did for your dad and the incredible comfort you were to me during the 5 months of his final illness. Lori and Chad, your excellent nursing skills were invaluable; Jerod, your medical knowledge kept your dad stable; and Datton, your quiet strength was a rock for me.

Many extended family members, personal friends, and acquaintances in my writing community prayed for us. Thank you a million times over. I felt those prayers!

Matthew and Mark, my amazing sons, you guys remained the light of my life throughout my first adjustment year after James passed, even though you were dealing with your own journeys through the grief process. Thank you for standing strong for your momma.

My publisher, Teresa Janzen, and Acquisitions Editor, Pastor Jenn Dafoe-Turner believed in this book and made it ready for its world debut. I'm so excited to be a part of the Abundance Books family and look forward the many more books we'll release together to minister to the planet.

And to my new husband, Michael J. Peterson: Thank you for gently allowing me to move into our new relationship. You build me up. You're my new king and you treat me like a queen.

Foreword

No matter who a woman is or what she does in her life, being a wife provides a rich and unique identity she freely assumes and lives. When she becomes a widow, that identity is ripped away. Yesterday she was one of two, part of a pair; now she is one.

What does she do with the love she used to give her husband? How does she fill the time she spent either with him or thinking about him? How does she adapt to a future she planned to spend with him and must now live alone?

Despite the 700,000 plus new widows each year in the United States, becoming/being a widow is an intensely personal and private thing. No one can relieve an aching woman of her grief and loneliness. Friends and family may love her, care for her, and be present with her, but only the widow herself knows the depth of her loss.

No more back rubs or arms around her shoulders. No more holding hands.

No more evenings going out to dinner or watching TV together.

No more sitting side by side in church.

No more arguments over money or time or politics.

No more debating when and where to vacation and how much to spend.

No more working together to raise the best kids possible.

No more toilet seats left up, toothpaste caps left off, or dirty dishes plopped in the sink with the expectation they will magically appear clean and sparkling in the cupboard.

And that's the merest tip of the iceberg of the "no mores" hidden beneath the ocean of a widow's tears.

Sharon Elliott has faced the dark nights and the aching loneliness.

Using material she wrote her first year without her beloved James, she invites us to journey with her through this introduction to life as a widow. Learn with her that you will survive. Rejoice with her in the comforting presence of the Lord who holds us widows in his loving arms through the depths of our pain. Discover with her that the Rock on which we stand is the sure foundation for our new and very different lives.

-Gayle Roper

A Widow's Journey; Prayers for a Widow's Journey

"Behold, I am doing a new thing. . ."
Isaiah 43:19

Letter to the Reader

I'm sure you've heard it over and over again, but it's absolutely true: I'm so sorry for your loss. My feelings, thoughts, complaints, and prayers have found their way into diaries and journals ever since I received my first little locking diary for my 12th birthday. All those pages carried me through every year of my life since then. So at the passing of my spiritual other half, writing out my grief was only natural.

After Him is a grief journey devotional you can work through at your own pace. Each chapter is divided into three days or segments. Perhaps you'll choose to deal with a chapter a month like I originally wrote most of the entries. The majority were Facebook posts written on the month-iversary of the day James passed. So, if your loved one died on the 5th, on the 5th of every month, you could read and journal Day 1. Two days later, maybe even a week later, you could read and journal Day 2, and two-three days later, you could read and journal Day 3. You could also go through this journal once a week, or haphazardly, just whenever you want to sit down to write. I'll give you some more ideas on Day 3 of Week 1.

Although you'll hear that phrase about your loss for the next few years, know that your husband is not lost. Your memories of him remain securely in your heart and in the hearts of everyone who knew and loved him. And his heart is secure in the arms of Jesus. Be comforted by the Spirit of God as you continue to live "after him."

~Sharon

Contents

Week One

Day One
At the Beginning of the Journey

From time to time, like Jacob, we will come upon moments when we too must wrestle with God. However, despite the obvious mix-match of the opponents—the Almighty God vs. puny us—we will miraculously survive, and when we come away from the match, three things will have taken place. First, our walk will be different because something has happened on the inside. Our understanding of God will have deepened enabling us to operate (walk) more circumspectly. Second, our name will be different. There will be an outer change. Our new gait—our limp—will be recognized as being associated with our encounter with God and others will begin to call us by the new identity God has given us. Third, we will go away from the experience blessed.

I know the above to be true, but my wrestle with God at the beginning of my husband James's cancer journey was more like a game of checkers, chess, or Stratego©. We made our moves trying to strategically look ahead to what God's next move might be. But unlike the board games, we were not trying to defeat our opponent, in fact, God was not an opponent but an ally, not playing against us, but traveling with us to whatever the end might be.

So, upon James's diagnosis of stage four liver cancer, he and I immediately set our hearts and minds on preparing for the day God would cure him. We made every move trying our best to read God's strategy so we could keep up with how He wanted us to manage what we were facing.

We decided to treat the news of James's diagnosis like we had grown to treat everything else in our lives—we would trust God with the unknown. We leaned on scripture. I wrote faith and healing scriptures on index cards and posted them around the house—on the doors, our desks, our headboards, and even on the TV tray James used in front of his favorite chair.

The first new place we had to visit was the cancer center and meet the doctor who would be handling James's case. James wanted to simply get down to brass tacks:

Explain the disease in simple terms that we could all understand.

What was the outlook?

What were the medications and their effectiveness in similar cases?

What was his life expectancy?

Once the answers were received, we struck out into the battle. Perhaps in a future publication, I'll tell all of what we encountered, how others figured into the fight, and what we learned from God's word. Suffice it to say for our current purpose that just five months later, we arrived at the end of our cancer journey when James slipped peacefully into Heaven.

Journal about the beginning of your journey. Look back and remember as much as you can about how it all started and how you felt at the time.

Week One: Day Two
Wrestling with God

And [Jacob] arose that night and took his two wives, his two female servants, and his eleven sons, and crossed over the ford of Jabbok. He took them, sent them over the brook, and sent over what he had. Then Jacob was left alone; and a Man wrestled with him until the breaking of day. Now when He saw that He did not prevail against him, He touched the socket of his hip; and the socket of Jacob's hip was out of joint as He wrestled with him. And He said, "Let Me go, for the day breaks."

But he said, "I will not let You go unless You bless me!"

So He said to him, "What is your name?"

He said, "Jacob."

And He said, "Your name shall no longer be called Jacob, but [i]Israel; for you have struggled with God and with men, and have prevailed."

Then Jacob asked, saying, "Tell me Your name, I pray."

And He said, "Why is it that you ask about My name?" And He blessed him there.

So Jacob called the name of the place [j]Peniel: "For I have seen God face to face, and my life is preserved." *[31]Just as he crossed over [k]Penuel the sun rose on him, and he limped on his hip. [32]Therefore to this day the children of Israel do not eat the muscle that shrank, which is on the hip socket, because He [l]touched the socket of Jacob's hip in the muscle that shrank.*

Genesis 32:22-32 (NIV)

Journal your reaction to the above passage as it relates to your wrestling with God at the beginning of your grief journey.

Week One: Day Three

When the sickness battle ends in death, another odyssey immediately begins—your personal grief journey. And that's why we're here. I am so very sorry for your loss, but now that you've walked your loved one Home, I'd like to walk with you through this first incredible year.

As I mentioned in the opening letter, you can work through this grief journey devotional at your own pace. Perhaps you'll choose to deal with this journal once a month like I originally wrote most of the entries. Or you can work through the book each week. This will allow you to not only get through the journal more quickly, but you will get an encouraging preview of what possibly is to come in your journey.

Finally, feel free to work through this book with a group. Some ideas of groups you could join or pioneer include:

A widows' fellowship group including women who are in caretaker positions with their husbands.

A group of your family members who are working through the loss of the same loved one but who may not be discussing their feelings and needs.

The couple's fellowship at your church or community center to boost appreciation of your spouse. These reflections could open what may be difficult conversations about final plans and wishes.

Journal your plans for working through this grief journey devotional. Include writing a letter to God in which you ask Him for revelation about the comfort and knowledge you'll receive as you work through this little book.

Week Two

Day One:
The Day He Died

The walk Home is done. My husband, Deacon James Elliott, has crossed over. He's actually seeing Jesus face-to-face! No more medicines, difficulty speaking, suffering from not being able to eat or walk or talk or take care of his own personal physical needs. No more cancer treatments followed by the bad news that "there's nothing more we can do." All that is real for James right now is the glory of Heaven and eternal life with God. Such a deal!

Like with every couple, we'd get exasperated with each other, but somehow, we were always able to get ourselves back together. We lived by the adage I suggest every couple should adopt. Tell each other, "If you leave me, I'm coming with you."

Well, I suppose James didn't really leave me this morning. He's simply doing what he always did—he's going before me. Always taking care of business! He was a pretty open book, so all who knew him, saw how he lived. One day, I'll tell you the story of how he was a shining example of how to die.

Thank you, friends, for continuing to pray for me and the rest of our family as we walk through this new world without James. I love you for holding my hands up.

30

Journal everything you can remember about the day your loved one died.

Week Two: Day Two
Holding Up My Hands

*Now Amalek came and fought with Israel in Rephidim.
And Moses said to Joshua, "Choose us some men and go
out, fight with Amalek. Tomorrow I will stand on the top
of the hill with the rod of God in my hand."*

*So Joshua did as Moses said to him, and fought with
Amalek. And Moses, Aaron, and Hur went up to the top
of the hill. And so it was, when Moses held up his hand,
that Israel prevailed; and when he let down his hand,
Amalek prevailed. But Moses' hands became heavy; so
they took a stone and put it under him, and he sat on
it. And Aaron and Hur supported his hands, one on
one side, and the other on the other side; and his hands
were steady until the going down of the sun. So Joshua
defeated Amalek and his people with the edge of the
sword.*

Exodus 17:8-13 (NKJV)

****

I thought I was in a battle as I did everything I could to take care
of James as he declined. But I had no idea what I would be in for when
James moved out (to Heaven) and grief moved in. Grief is a much
more difficult patient—invisible, demanding, unrelenting. I needed
others to join me in the fight to get through it. Either grief would win
and overwhelm me, or otherworldly Godly strength would win and
keep me going. I was tired, so friends and family members from near
and far fought in prayer for me and for the latter to win. They have
figuratively held my hands up while the war ensued. During hard days
when I languished at home alone, someone would literally text or
email me saying, "Hello there. How are you doing today? You've been
on my mind." I'd tell the person about my day, and she'd write back,
"No wonder God put you on my mind. I'm praying."

Those prayers would be like getting a check in the mail when you're down to your last dime. Those prayers almost tactilely hugged me. And those who spoke words of encouragement often said exactly what I needed to hear—they were the voice of God at that precise moment.

Yes, I was vulnerable. If you had asked me how I felt and what I was going through, you would have received an earful. How else would my friends know the truth and how to help me?

Journal your reaction to the above passage as it relates to "having your hands held up." Did anyone help you the day your husband died or during the immediate days that followed? How so? If you did not have help, why not? How did you encourage or discourage interactions with others? Did you encourage yourself in healthy or unhealthy ways?

Week Two: Day Three

I'm so very sorry for your loss! My experience included five months from James's diagnosis of stage four liver cancer to his transition from earth to Heaven. Because he was so well-loved by family and friends, coupled with my previous connections made via a mission trip and a globally watched internet TV show, people from all over the world were praying for James's healing on this side of Glory. Still, his health continued to decline. During his final three weeks, with the incredible support of his grown children, I was able to have him home for his hospice care. Then on Tuesday morning, May 16, at 12:50 a.m., he drew his final breath of our atmosphere's air and his first one of The Holy City's—that is, if our new bodies need to breathe!

I don't know how long I cried after he was transported to the mortuary, but I remember it being a beautiful day and marveling about how the world outside just kept moving along despite the devastating drama playing out behind my door. Shouldn't the world be still and reverent right now? Shouldn't it be cloudy and raining?

Taking care of "things" now had to happen. Although thankfully we had a living trust in place and James's instructions explaining exactly what he wanted me to do, the execution of the trust and those plans needed to be overseen. Having the living trust in place, holding James's handwritten funeral service plan, and reflecting on the memories of how I knew he wanted things done still did not fully prepare me for the emptiness I felt inside without the man with whom I had become one. Literally, a part of me—the part he filled—had died. He was gone. It was final and permanent. At the drop of a hat, tears just came, but I couldn't just check out. There was work to do.

Journal a prayer about your immediate concerns now that your husband has passed away? Write out your thoughts. You can use this space to organize your time and tasks. Feel free to use this space as both a dumping ground for your feelings, but also as your to-do list.

(For your convenience, look over the list provided in the glossary to see items that must now be handled when death takes our husbands away.)

Week Three

Day One
Between His Death and the Homegoing Celebration

Frankly, this week and a half went by in a blur. It felt as if I was just putting one foot in front of the other. I planned the memorial service to be held at our church and chose to have James's body there, up front, in his coffin so that friends and family members could get closure by saying their final goodbyes. At the writing of this book, I guess that's becoming an old-fashioned way of celebrating a memorial service. Many people are choosing cremation because it is so much less expensive than paying for mortuary services, a casket, and space in a cemetery. (Different faiths and denominations hold varying views about cremation. Check the glossary of this book for a quick review of some of the major points of view on the subject.)

In order to get the information about the service out to everyone who would possibly have wanted to attend, I posted the following announcement on all my social media sites:

Hello Family and Friends,

I miss James SOOO much and I am looking forward to celebrating him and seeing all of you in person at James's homegoing celebration this Friday, May 26, at 10am (9am viewing) Christ Second Baptist Church,

1471 Martin Luther King Jr. Ave., Long Beach, CA.

 However, if it's impossible for you to make it in person, join us on Zoom. Here is the link…

Journal about whether or not you are planning a memorial event. If that time is behind you, journal your remembrances of planning that day and what happened on that day and at the service.

Week Three: Day Two

Now it was about the sixth hour, and there was darkness over all the earth until the ninth hour. Then the sun was darkened, and the veil of the temple was torn in two. And when Jesus had cried out with a loud voice, He said, "Father, 'into Your hands I commit My spirit.' " Having said this, He breathed His last.

So when the centurion saw what had happened, he glorified God, saying, "Certainly this was a righteous Man!"

And the whole crowd who came together to that sight, seeing what had been done, beat their breasts and returned. But all His acquaintances, and the women who followed Him from Galilee, stood at a distance, watching these things.

Now behold, there was a man named Joseph, a council member, a good and just man. He had not consented to their decision and deed. He was from Arimathea, a city of the Jews, who himself was also waiting for the kingdom of God. This man went to Pilate and asked for the body of Jesus. Then he took it down, wrapped it in linen, and laid it in a tomb that was hewn out of the rock, where no one had ever lain before. That day was the Preparation, and the Sabbath drew near.

And the women who had come with Him from Galilee followed after, and they observed the tomb and how His body was laid. Then they returned and prepared spices and fragrant oils. And they rested on the Sabbath according to the commandment.

Luke 23:44-55

Journal your reaction to the above passage as it relates to the disposition of your husband's body and the truth that his resurrection lies ahead. Your husband's tomb, urn, or even scattered ashes are wherever they are for safekeeping until Jesus returns.

Week Three: Day Three

Journal a prayer to God in which you talk with Him about the memorial service, burial, cremation, disposition of ashes, or whatever other way you chose your husband's final resting place. Maybe you did not have the opportunity to choose that place or have a memorial service. Talk to God about that.

Week Four

Day One
It's Been a Month; I Miss Him So Much

It's been a month since my husband, James Elliott, has been gone. I miss him terribly. Your very sincere and impassioned pleas to God for James's healing were not in vain. Love radiates from the soul and spirit. The man I loved and who loved me is completely healed although his body never got better. So, since his body wouldn't cooperate with the prayers, he left it behind and moved to where the real James could live an eternally healthy life.

James loved and enjoyed life, his family, and his friends, and left here with no regrets, not because he was perfect, but because he had trusted Christ as his Savior. To the best of his ability, James had done what God wanted him to do. He had carried out his responsibilities and had humbled himself to obey God's word.

In church, when we were led in prayer, James would reach over and take my hand. We'd hold hands as we stood with the rest of the congregation before God's throne. We didn't hold hands at other times—just when we were before God. Throughout the day on May 15th, one month ago, we held hands as he prepared to go to the throne room in person. He got there in the early morning hours of May 16th.

James, my hands can no longer be wrapped in yours. I miss your grip that always reassured me. As I've always been, I'm in God's hands, but I'm in His hands without you. I miss you, Honey. Have fun!

Journal about how you and your husband celebrated your faith as a couple.

Week Four: Day Two

Be sure to know—and live for—Jesus for yourself. Many don't think it's important to be mindful of the reality of Heaven and hell. However, after witnessing my dear husband's transition from this world to the next—Heaven for him for certain—I am more dedicated than ever to compel you to secure your relationship with God through Jesus Christ. Read John 3:16 and Romans 10:6-10 and govern yourself accordingly.

****

For God so loved the world that He gave His only begotten Son, that whoever believes in Him should not perish but have everlasting life.

John 3:16

But the righteousness of faith speaks in this way, "Do not say in your heart, 'Who will ascend into Heaven?' " (that is, to bring Christ down from above) or, " 'Who will descend into the abyss?' " (that is, to bring Christ up from the dead). But what does it say? "The word is near you, in your mouth and in your heart" (that is, the word of faith which we preach): that if you confess with your mouth the Lord Jesus and believe in your heart that God has raised Him from the dead, you will be saved. For with the heart one believes unto righteousness, and with the mouth confession is made unto salvation.

Romans 10:6-10

****

For more information, contact me at LifeThatMatters@yahoo.com if you want to talk more about salvation.

Journal your reaction to the above passages as they relate to salvation. How are you feeling about your faith in light of what you've been through and the grief you are experiencing?

Week Four: Day Three

Journal: Perhaps you are reading this when it's been about a month since your husband's passing. As you look back on the decisions he made concerning his faith and the decisions you have made concerning yours, journal your thoughts in the form of a prayer to God.

Week Five

Day One
Thank You

Hello Family and Friends,

Thank you a million times over for all the love and support you have shown to my family and me during this ordeal of seeing my beloved husband, James Elliott, through his illness and journey to Glory. God has used your outpouring of concern to hold me up. I am grateful for every beautiful card (I read them all and displayed them on my dining room table), and every gift which either has been or will be put to good use. I look forward to continuing our friendship and working in the Kingdom together. James would not want us to function in any other way.

Ablaze,

Sharon

****

I placed the above note on Facebook because there were people from many states and even a few countries who had been praying for me. No matter how busy I got, I didn't want to forget the kindness others were showing to me.

Perhaps you had to go through this terrible ordeal alone. I am so sorry if that was your experience. Know that God has not left you alone and He never will.

Whether you are going through this season with lots of human friends or alone with the Master of the universe, believe it or not, there are still things and situations for which to be thankful.

Journal your reaction to the above reflection as it relates to being thankful at this time in your widowhood.

Week Five: Day Two

The Scripture passage below is taken from Colossians chapter 3. How interesting that the subheading in my Bible labels these verses as "Character of the New Man," the word "man" being used to refer to humankind—both men and women. That's what we are now as widows—we are new women. Although I chose this passage to focus on thankfulness, the rest of the passage gives us many other characteristics upon which to focus.

****

Therefore, as the elect of God, holy and beloved, put on tender mercies, kindness, humility, meekness, longsuffering; bearing with one another, and forgiving one another, if anyone has a complaint against another; even as Christ forgave you, so you also must do. But above all these things put on love, which is the bond of perfection. And let the peace of God rule in your hearts, to which also you were called in one body; and **be thankful.** *Let the word of Christ dwell in you richly in all wisdom, teaching and admonishing one another in psalms and hymns and spiritual songs, singing with grace in your hearts to the Lord.*

Colossians 3:12-16 NKJ
(Bold italics added)

****

We have been spending time concentrating on the tears which are probably still leaking out every so often. Please know, that's okay. Tears tend to well up and drip over my lower lids at the most unexpected times—passing his favorite restaurant, seeing a car like his, hearing his favorite song on the radio. Go ahead and let those memories linger, but let's spend some time building the qualities listed in this passage, including thankfulness, God still intends for us to exude toward others.

Journal your reaction to the above passage as it relates to being thankful at this time in your widowhood. Also, see the glossary that includes a worksheet you can use if you decide to shift your focus to the building or adding of the characteristics of the new woman listed in Colossians 3:12-16.

Week Five: Day Three

What are your true thoughts about thankfulness or thanksgiving as you face this time of your widow's journey? Is it easy or hard to feel thankful?

Journal: Be honest with God about your feelings and journal your thoughts in the form of a prayer to Him.

Week Six

Day One
First Holidays After Him

They say (whoever "they" are) the first year after a loved one's passing is the hardest when facing each "first" holiday. Well, here we are at the first holiday after James's departure. For me, that holiday is Father's Day. James had actually planned for this Father's Day to mark his return the church. Instead, he went to God's real house!

Happy Father's Day to James and my daddy, Vincent Norris. By now, the two have probably met. Maybe my daddy would want to know if James had taken good care of me. James will be able to give him a good report!

Then quickly approaching after Father's Day would have been our 22nd wedding anniversary. We liked commemorating our special days. For example, our first date was March 8th. That date was so significant to us that we went out for a special dinner every year to remember how it all began. We'd rehearse the best times of that date and talk about what had led up to it. You see, we had met through a dating service; not one through which we used the computer to meet, but one that required us to physically go into the office for the interview, to fill out paperwork, to take professional photos, and record a video. Then we were required to go back in periodically to check to see if someone had expressed interest.

Desiring to always live by the principles of the Bible, I had consulted with God about whether He was okay with this form of meeting. After all, Proverbs 18:22 says, "He who finds a wife finds a good thing, and obtains favor from the Lord." Was I pushing the envelope by being the one trying to do the "finding"? God comforted my heart, though, by reminding me that I couldn't be "found" unless I was at places where there would be single men. And as it turned out, God even took care of that little concern for me. Even though I looked through all the men's profiles, somehow, I didn't see James. His profile was definitely in the book because he had joined the dating service before I had. So, James did indeed "find" me!

Journal your remembrances about the first couple of holidays or special days you are experiencing without your "him." Are there any happy memories your heart and mind can rehearse?

Week Six: Day Two

The Bible is full of verses and passages that talk about remembering. Interestingly enough, sometimes the verses tell us about God doing the remembering. For example, the rainbow is God's sign about which He says it will remind Him of His own covenant never to destroy the whole earth by flood again. (See Genesis 9:16.) It is also said that God "remembered" the relationship He had with Abraham, so that's why He rescued Lot (Abraham's nephew) from Sodom before He destroyed the whole city. (See Genesis 19:29).

Now don't get it twisted, God is not suffering from dementia. He knows us, remembers his promises to us, and carries out His love toward us every minute of every single day. He does not forget anything but our sin which He mercifully tosses into the sea of forgetfulness:

****

Who is a God like You, pardoning iniquity and passing over the transgression of the remnant of His heritage? He does not retain His anger forever, because He delights in mercy. He will again have compassion on us, and will subdue our iniquities. You will cast all our sins into the depths of the sea.

Micah 7:18-19 NKJ

****

The Word of God also talks about that which we ought to remember. Exodus 13:3 told the Children of Israel to "remember this day in which you went out of Egypt, out of the house of bondage; for by strength of hand the Lord brought you out of this place. No leavened bread shall be eaten." This command led to the institution of the

Feast of Unleavened Bread, which is a celebration of remembrance of the day God delivered them from Egyptian bondage. Every year they were to remember what God had done.

Just like the annual Christian remembrances of Christmas and Easter remind of us of Jesus' advent and resurrection, we ought to be regularly calling to mind all that God has done and all He means to us. Psalm 20:6-8 declares,:

> *Now I know that the Lord saves His anointed;*
>
> *He will answer him from His holy Heaven with the*
> *saving strength of His right hand. Some trust in chariots,*
> *and some in horses; but* we will remember *the name of*
> *the Lord our God. They have bowed down and fallen;*
> *but we have risen and stand upright.*

Psalm 20:6-8
(Bold italics added)

My friend Teresa's dad, Dr. Fred Campbell, always says he has "a robust romance with the Redeemer." Even in our widowhood, we can regularly remember and celebrate the robust romance we too experience with our Savior.

Journal your reaction to the above comments and verses about remembering.

Week Six: Day Three

The memories you have of your husband may be sweet; however, very few people have no faults. You may find yourself recalling the realities of the bitter words or moments of your marriage. That's okay. You are not disrespecting his memory by allowing the tough stretches of your relationship to surface.

In the movie *Kingdom Come,* Whoopi Goldberg plays a widow by the name of Raynelle Slocumb. In speaking about her late husband with her pastor as she prepares for the funeral, Rev. Hooker tells her, "In my experience, it's best to remember the happier times."

Raynelle responds, "Well, they were few and far between. He was mean and surly." (*Kingdom Come*, 2001. Directed by Doug McHenry. Starring and ensemble cast including Whoopi Goldberg, LL Cool J, Jada Pinkett Smith, Anthony Anderson, etc.)

It's time to be free of the pain the sour memories have caused. You may have buried your hurts because, for some reason, you didn't want your husband to know about them. You may now be realizing you were not operating out of respect but out of fear. You no longer have to live that way.

First John 4:18 comforts us with these words:

There is no fear in love; but perfect love casts out fear, because fear involves torment. But he who fears has not been made perfect in love.

1st John 4:18 NKJ

****

Place your fear of fully expressing yourself in the hands of Jesus. Ask Him to release you from the muffler that has silenced your ability to speak up for yourself. Then request that He help you know how to stay free as you learn to express yourself in a way that honors your freedom as a human being, yet doesn't come across as arrogance or bitterness toward others.

There's also nothing wrong with basking in the sweet memories you have of your husband. I relish the opportunities I get to talk about the wonderful parts of my life with James. It makes me smile (and probably still blush) when I tell someone about how he used to wink at me in church, or flash his sly grin and eye twinkle when he asked, "Did I tell you 'I love you' today?'" Recalling the private moments make me grin too—as well they should. My James was quite the charmer!

Retelling your wonderful love story is a healthy part of your grief recovery, a great way to make you start feeling better, and just a start to what can bring hope to another widow.

Journal a prayer to God in which you talk with Him about both the sour and sweet memories of your relationship with your late husband. No matter how you start, do your best to end with the sweet ones.

Week Seven

Day One
Alone with Myself and my Thoughts

Three months ago, on May 16th at 12:50am, you quietly slipped from this life to the next. I'll never forget your last shallow breath. I miss you so much. I so wanted you to get better, and you did, but you had to leave your body to do it. I miss holding hands. I miss laying my head on your chest listening to your heartbeat. I miss discussions about politics and whatever caught your eye in the L.A. Times (that you read cover-to-cover every day.)

Life without you is so different. I don't feel empty because I have Jesus, purpose, and hope, but I used to have you to share all of life with. Without a shadow of a doubt, I know you loved me, and I have amazing memories of our life both at home and on vacations, so I'm grateful. Some people never get to experience a love like ours. God blessed us and now it's incredibly lonely without you.

By the way, the new TV you bought me stopped working. You always handled such problems. Now I've gotta call "the guy" to come fix it.

I love you, Honey.

Journal about missing your husband. What's going on in your emotions? How are you handling "alone"? How are you spending your time? Write about your thought life.

Week Seven: Day Two

Sometimes, our thought life can get out of control when we're alone. What should we do about that? First of all, it's always a good idea to remind ourselves that in actuality, we are not alone. God's word tells us:

> *Blessed is the man whom You instruct, O Lord, and teach out of Your law, that You may give him rest from the days of adversity, until the pit is dug for the wicked. For the Lord will not cast off His people,* nor will He forsake His inheritance.

Psalm 94:12-14
(Bold italics added)

We're comforted by the words of the Old Testament, especially by lots of the entries in the collection of the psalms. However, sometimes we just want to hear Jesus' voice speak to our hearts. A huge swath of the book of John in the Bible is attributed to have been spoken by Jesus Himself. In fact, if you own a red-letter Bible in which Jesus' actual words are indicated by being printed in red, chapters 10 – 17 are almost all red. Hearing Jesus say He'll always be with me, spoken in first person, has had a special, powerful effect. Look at John 14:16-18:

> *And I will pray the Father, and He will give you another Helper, that He may abide with you forever—the Spirit of truth, whom the world cannot receive, because it neither sees Him nor knows Him; but you know Him, for He dwells with you and will be in you.* I will not leave you orphans; *I will come to you.*

John 14:16-18
(Bold italics added)

****

Once our minds are settled on the reality that Jesus will never leave us, how do we handle the rest of the thoughts that fly through our heads? Obviously, we need to think about practical things related to getting through every day. There are thousands of other healthy things to think about as well—marvelous things like the beauty of our world, the wonder of new discoveries, and the people we love. Second Corinthians 10:3-6 instructs us about our lives and our thought life:

> *For though we walk in the flesh, we do not war according to the flesh. For the weapons of our warfare are not carnal but* **mighty in God for pulling down strongholds,** *casting down arguments and every high thing that exalts itself against the knowledge of God,* bringing *every thought into captivity to the obedience of Christ, and being ready to punish all disobedience when your obedience is fulfilled.*

Corinthians 10:3-6 (NKJ)
(Bold italics added)

The Message version of the Bible paraphrases this passage beautifully:

> *The world is unprincipled. It's dog-eat-dog out there! The world doesn't fight fair. But we don't live or fight our battles that way—never have and never will. The tools of our trade aren't for marketing or manipulation, but they are for demolishing that entire massively corrupt culture. We use our powerful God-tools for smashing warped philosophies, tearing down barriers erected against the truth of God, fitting every loose thought and emotion and impulse into the structure of life shaped by Christ. Our tools are ready at hand for clearing the ground of every obstruction and building lives of obedience into maturity.*

(Bold italics added)

Journal your reaction to the above passages as they relate to missing your husband and your present thought life.

Week Seven: Day Three

By this point in my grief journey, as if it hadn't been enough to get used to being labeled a "widow," I now began to really come to terms with the word "alone." My eyes were still filling with tears at unexpected moments, and as executor of James's trust, my attention was still turning daily to the business of that document's execution. Just as I hadn't known how long we'd live, or how long James's illness would linger, I now had no idea how long this business of wrapping up James's death would continue—both legally on paper, and emotionally in my heart.

Journal and tell God in prayer about how you are handling "alone."

Week Eight

Day One
Your Next Meeting

It's been 5 months since I had to let go of his hand. I miss him SO much. James made my life sweet and secure. He never stopped winking at me and flirting with me. He made me blush for 21 years. I can only imagine what he's doing in Glory right now, and what a ride it will be when his space at Inglewood Park Cemetery becomes the Rapture Shoot for his resurrected body when the trumpet of First Thessalonians 5:16-17 sounds! Although the ache of separation lingers with me, I always wanted him surrounded with peace, love, and joy. Our home here was such a place; now he's eternally in the peace, joy, and love of Heaven.

****

After writing the above Facebook entry, I realized I had not dreamt about James. I am living in the gap either between his death and mine, or between his death and the Rapture. Soon enough, though, I experienced my first dream about James. We were leaving church and I had stopped to talk with some visitors after the service. When I turned from them, James was patiently waiting, sitting cross-legged on the pavement (which he had never done fearing he wouldn't be able to get up). As I approached, he indicated that he wanted me to ride home with him. I was wondering how we would get both cars home as we had driven separately to church that morning. Before I could ask, a young lady we knew passed by. James pulled me toward him in a hug, kissed me twice, and flashed his smile at her. "I bet you wish you had the kind of love we have!"

Of course, I blushed and looked up at James's face. Then I woke up.

Journal if you've had any dreams about your "him" as you have slept, record them here.

Week Eight: Day Two

Did you know that every chapter in the book of First Thessalonians speaks of the Rapture of the Church?

… how you turned to God from idols to serve the living and true God, and to wait for His Son from Heaven, whom He raised from the dead, even Jesus who delivers us from the wrath to come.

I Thessalonians 1:9b-10

For what is our hope, or joy, or crown of rejoicing? Is it not even you in the presence of our Lord Jesus Christ at His coming?

I Thessalonians 2:19

And may the Lord make you increase and abound in love to one another and to all, just as we do to you, so that He may establish your hearts blameless in holiness before our God and Father at the coming of our Lord Jesus Christ with all His saints.

I Thessalonians 3:12-13

For the Lord Himself will descend from Heaven with a shout, with the voice of an archangel, and with the trumpet of God. And the dead in Christ will rise first. 17 Then we who are alive and remain shall be caught up together with them in the clouds to meet the Lord in the air. And thus we shall always be with the Lord.

I Thessalonians 4:16-17

But concerning the times and the seasons, brethren, you have no need that I should write to you. For you yourselves know perfectly that the day of the Lord so comes as a thief in the night… But you, brethren, are not in darkness, so that this Day should overtake you as a thief.

I Thessalonians 5:1-2, 4

****

What's the Rapture? You ask good questions! The Billy Graham Evangelistic Association succinctly explains the Rapture on its website:

There are many Christians who believe that the second coming of Jesus Christ will be in two phases. First, He will come for believers, both living and dead, in the "rapture" (read 1 Thessalonians 4:13-17). In this view, the rapture—which is the transformation and catching up of all Christians, dead or alive, to meet Christ in the air—will be secret, for it will be unknown to the world of unbelievers at the time of its happening.

The effect of this removal, in the absence of multitudes of people, will, of course, be evident on earth. Then, second, after a period of seven years of tribulation on earth, Christ will return to the earth with His church, the saints who were raptured (Matthew 24:30, 2 Thessalonians 1:7, 1 Peter 1:13, Revelation 1:7). He will be victorious over His enemies and will reign on the earth for 1,000 years (the millennium) with His saints, the church.

https://billygraham.org/answer/what-is-the-rapture/

****

Even if you are not from a Christian tradition that ascribes to a belief in the Rapture of the Church, both Catholic and Protestant denominations look expectantly forward to the Second Coming of our Lord Jesus. If you and your "him" are believers, your future includes a reunion in Glory. The good news is that despite differences you may have had in this life, Heaven is a place of peace and rest where strife and misunderstandings will all be put aside.

Journal your reaction to the Rapture of the Church or the Second Coming and about looking forward to reuniting with your "him" in Glory.

Week Eight: Day Three

Journal: Do you feel you are ready for the Rapture or the Second Coming? Talk with God in prayer about your own readiness. What is God's purpose for you now that you're without your "him"?

Week Nine

Day One
Heaven is Real

James has been experiencing Heaven for 6 months today. I know he's not bored, and I often wonder what he's doing. What was it like to tell Jesus face-to-face that he loved him? What did he do when Jesus introduced him to God the Father? Did the Holy Spirit meet James at the entrance? James liked his gold jewelry. How is he enjoying walking on the golden streets? I miss him so much, but he must be having an incredible time!

****

Reading back over these entries reminded me of the first thing I said to James when I realized he had taken his final breath. As the reality of the moment hit me, I said to him, "You're looking at Jesus right now!"

Everything I've lived to believe about God, Jesus Christ, the Holy Spirit, and Heaven rushed in on me at that moment. All I have dedicated my life to—my Christian college experience; my 35+ years teaching in Christian schools; my hours listening to sermons, studying my Bible, and memorizing Scripture; my determination to raise my children to love the Lord; my current business and ministry—came into sharp focus right then.

Journal: Discuss with God any doubts you have about Him and/or the afterlife. If you have no doubts, journal about why you're so sure.

Week Nine: Day Two

John 14:1-6 is one of the most reassuring passages in the Bible about the afterlife. Jesus wanted His disciples (and us by extension) to maintain their hope although He would soon be going to the Cross. At the time, the disciples could not fathom the Lord leaving them, much less being murdered. Let Jesus encourage you today with the same words He spoke back then:

> Let not your heart be troubled; you believe in God, believe also in Me. In My Father's house are many mansions; if it were not so, I would have told you. I go to prepare a place for you. And if I go and prepare a place for you, I will come again and receive you to Myself; that where I am, there you may be also. And where I go you know, and the way you know." Thomas said to Him, "Lord, we do not know where You are going, and how can we know the way?" Jesus said to him, "I am the way, the truth, and the life. No one comes to the Father except through Me.

John 14:1-6

Thankfully, Jesus' absence from his disciples only lasted three days. In His resurrection, He triumphed over death. No other faith's religious leader is a living Savior. Hallelujah!

Journal your reaction to the above passage as it relates to Jesus being your way, your truth, and your life.

Week Nine: Day Three

When I was a little girl in Sunday school, I loved singing the songs we were taught. One of them was a simple little chorus about Heaven:

> Heaven is a wonderful place.
>
> Filled with glory and grace.
>
> I'm gonna see my Savior's face.
>
> Yes, Heaven is a wonder place.

Journal: Speak first person to God discussing what you know about His place. Let God know your thankfulness about your secure future and how you feel about Heaven.

Week Ten

Day One
Life is Now Different

Today, Dec. 16th, marked the 7th month since James graduated to Heaven. Memories of preparing for Christmas over the years flooded my mind all day. He had the spiritual gift of giving but he allowed that to roll over to his personal gift giving. He was the best! He'd plan for months, research for the best price, and search for the exact item I'd been wanting or needing but hadn't even asked for.

We talked on the phone for a month and a half, met for the first time in person in March, and were married in August. Christmas came before we had known each other for a year. Regardless of that short time frame, he had listened and watched as I traveled several times to conferences that had something to do with my writing and speaking. So, for that first Christmas, James bought me a new set of luggage so I could travel in style! Other gifts followed that I didn't ask for but which he knew I would appreciate because of my business, like the lightweight power point projector and the large screen Apple computer.

****

At the writing of his section, I just realized it took five months for us to get married, and five months to navigate through his illness and departure. What a coincidence. Even with the ups and downs, the twenty-one years in between welded us together as a strong, loving unit.

During the first year after your husband's death, there may be no one in your life caring for you as he had done, so you get to focus on making Christmas special for someone else. A widow's first Christmas may mean she's spending Christmas Eve and Christmas morning alone for the first time in many, many years. Besides yourself, do you know another widow who needs gifts under her tree? Make it a merry Christmas for her. Go over to her home and spend part of Christmas Eve playing a board game or putting a puzzle together. Help her trim her tree and decorate her front door. Send her several beautifully-wrapped gifts so she'll have gifts to open on Christmas morning. A snuggly blanket she can wrap in while watching TV, a bead bracelet in her favorite color, a new pair of earrings, or some sweet-smelling shower gel could be great choices!

You can also uplift another widow for her first birthday, first Mothers' Day, or the first time remembering her anniversary without her husband.

Journal: What can you do for other widows as they face some memory milestones? Write down a list of the names of widows you know. Find out when their birthdays and anniversaries are and plan to send cards or give little gifts to them on those days.

Week Ten: Day Two

You are probably discovering how different the world, and your place in the world, seems now. Caring for yourself emotionally is of utmost importance as you discover just how different your world is without your "him." Several Scriptures that speak about change are able to encourage us.

****

¹To everything there is a season,

A time for every purpose under heaven:

²A time to be born, and a time to die;

A time to plant, and a time to pluck what is planted;

³A time to kill, and a time to heal;

A time to break down, and a time to build up;

⁴A time to weep, and a time to laugh;

A time to mourn, and a time to dance;

⁵A time to cast away stones, and a time to gather stones;

A time to embrace, and a time to refrain from embracing;

⁶A time to gain, and a time to lose;

A time to keep, and a time to throw away;

⁷A time to tear, and a time to sew;

A time to keep silence, and a time to speak;

⁸A time to love, and a time to hate;

A time of war, and a time of peace.

⁹What profit has the worker from that in which he labors? ¹⁰I have seen the God-given task with which

*the sons of men are to be occupied. ¹¹He has made
everything beautiful in its time.*

Ecclesiastes 3:1-11

****

*Behold, I will do a new thing, now it shall spring forth; shall you not
know it? I will even make a road in the wilderness and rivers in the
desert.*

Isaiah 43:19

****

*For I know the thoughts that I think toward you, says the Lord, thoughts
of peace and not of evil, to give you a future and a hope.*

Jeremiah 29:11

****

*For I know the thoughts that I think toward you, says the Lord, thoughts
of peace and not of evil, to give you a future and a hope.*

Hebrews 13:8

Journal: With the above Scriptures in mind, journal here discussing
your feelings and thoughts as they relate to God's promises and the
adjustments you have had to make as a widow.

Week Ten: Day Three

God is aware of each and every change we are going through as widows. He has not forgotten us. In fact, caring for widows is so important to God that He made sure the brand-new Church after the Resurrection addressed this as its very first issue. (See Acts chapter 6)

Journal a prayer to God, talking to Him about the adjustments you're forced to make now that you are a widow.

Week Eleven

Day One
Being Friendly

Merry Christmas to my Facebook family! You have held me up through your prayers this year and I sincerely appreciate every time you took me with you to the throne. Sunday morning during church, a wave of hot he's-not-here tears surprised me (as they do occasionally) and flooded in during one of the songs. However, the sermon, "Family Matters" delivered by Minister Roz, snapped me back. I'm a member of the family of God for which Jesus came.

My friend Tammy helped me with my Christmas tree. I wanted to share it with you. Some friends made sure I'd have some gifts under it for Christmas morning! So sweet and thoughtful!

Well, I need to get to bed. I have a big day tomorrow entertaining my extended family for Christmas dinner at my house in my newly remodeled space. I'll send you pictures after they see it in person for the first time.

Again, Merry Christmas! I love you.

Ablaze,

Sharon

****

I'll admit it: I had never spent time thinking about how widows would feel at Christmas time. I think I just assumed they would be with other members of their families—mainly their children. It took this experience to tenderize my heart toward this often-lonely segment of the population. Now that I was on the receiving side of alone, I know the feeling of that pain.

Several of my girlfriends really came through for me, though, making Christmas not only bearable but also wonderful. Once I vocalized the observation that for the first time in my life, I'd be alone on Christmas morning, probably with no gifts under my tree, they made Santa's wheels begin spinning. Within days, I started receiving deliveries on my porch. Then Tammy dropped everything she was doing and spent a whole day with me shopping for new ornaments, pulling the Christmas tree out of my storage room, and setting it up. Before long, I was singing, "It's beginning to look a lot like Christmas, everywhere you go." Those gift deliveries had a lovely place to be displayed until Christmas morning when I delightfully unwrapped them and took pictures with each one to send to my friends with the thank you notes.

Journal: Write down some plans you'd like to accomplish with your friends. Date the plans so they actually happen.

Week Eleven: Day Two

It's a strange phenomenon to move from being part of a couple to being single again. If you married when you were young, you probably built couple friendships over the years. You still know all those couples and they know you, but now the dynamic has changed. The same social events are happening, but now you could begin to feel like the odd man out. I've even heard that sometimes, the wives in the friend group become a bit jealous of a newly single woman, sometimes taking their jealousy as far as to accuse the single lady of having designs on their husbands.

I began to realize our society leans toward couples. Many amusement park rides are built for two people to sit side-by-side. Movies and dinner are standard date-night activities.

Thankfully, several decades ago when I married James, I kept up with my friends, whether they were married or single. And it didn't matter if my single sisters had never been married, were divorced, or had been widowed. Although there had been a couple of years toward the end of James's life when concentrating on him took more of my time than usual, those years did not erase the sisterhoods. After he died, not only was my time for them freed up, but some of the ladies from church—Ophelia, Debbie, and Gwen—who hung out together began inviting me to join their friend group and my life expanded to be able to include those lovely women as well.

Even though you are now a widow, you are still alive and well, and you have lots to contribute as a friend. Here are some verses from Scripture to encourage you to reach out and enjoy your friendships.

****

A friend loves at all times, and a brother is born for adversity.

Proverbs 17:17

****

Ointment and perfume delight the heart and the sweetness of a man's friend gives delight by hearty counsel.

Proverbs 27:9

****

This is My commandment, that you love one another as I have loved you. Greater love has no one than this, than to lay down one's life for his friends. You are My friends if you do whatever I command you. No longer do I call you servants, for a servant does not know what his master is doing; but I have called you friends, for all things that I heard from My Father I have made known to you.

John 15:12-15
(Bold italics added)

****

Therefore comfort each other and edify one another, just as you also are doing.

I Thessalonians 5:11

****

Rejoice with those who rejoice, and weep with those who weep.

Romans 12:15

****

A man who has friends must himself be friendly.

Proverbs 18:24a

Journal your reaction to the above Scriptures. How do they relate to you and your friendships? If any of them challenge you, contemplate why you feel challenged and write down what you plan to do to overcome the challenges.

Week Eleven: Day Three

Possibly the most challenging of the above Scriptures is Proverbs 18:24a because it's requiring something of us. At first, we may have felt uncomfortable being consoled; however, all too soon, the consolation wanes and the time comes to get back to the regular ebb and flow of life. A lifeline when we feel we're sinking is often thrown from friends. And we can throw some lifelines to other women, rescuing them from despair and loneliness by offering our friendship to them.

Journal a prayer to God asking Him to direct you toward friends who you need and friendships He wants you to develop. Discuss with Him how those friendships can be developed and/or strengthened.

Week Twelve

Day One
Don't Worry; Celebrate Today

I called him "Honey." He called me "Baby" (and another private nickname usually accompanied by a wink). The slight smile always meant there was something sweet and a bit racy on his mind. He could always make my heart flutter and my cheeks blush. Today would have been his 81st birthday, but he escaped having birthdays anymore because there's no such thing as getting old in Heaven!

We were told of the start of his life-ending journey the day before his birthday last year and we were granted 5 months to walk it out. Losing my Love was not a clean separation along a perforated line—it was a ripping apart that left a gaping hole in the fabric of my life. God, the Master tailor, is stitching the tear, making a beautiful design on my life using lasting memories with His skilled embroidery. Life is definitely different without James, but it can be and will be amazing because I'll never be without God.

So as my Honey celebrates his forever, I'll continue to celebrate our memories and my every day continuing opportunities to live life to the fullest (just as James did), loving and serving God, and basking in His love for me.

Whatever losses you may be feeling, please celebrate the hours, days, and years you shared. Let those times propel you rather than pull you down. I'm better, stronger, and wiser because I was James Elliott's wife for 21 years, and that's nothing to cry about!

Journal: Describe at least two or three things you can celebrate about today. I'm in His hands without you. I miss you, Honey. Have fun!

Week Twelve: Day Two

During Biblical days, most women were entirely dependent upon the men in their lives to care for them. As single women, they lived with and were cared for by their fathers. Once married, their husbands took on the responsibility of their upkeep. So, when her husband died, and there was no one else in the family able to take her in, that widow could become destitute. Read two of the Bible's widow stories:

****

Story #1: A Widow and Her Sons

A certain woman of the wives of the sons of the prophets cried out to Elisha, saying, "Your servant my husband is dead, and you know that your servant feared the Lord. And the creditor is coming to take my two sons to be his slaves."

So Elisha said to her, "What shall I do for you? Tell me, what do you have in the house?" And she said, "Your maidservant has nothing in the house but a jar of oil."

Then he said, "Go, borrow vessels from everywhere, from all your neighbors—empty vessels; do not gather just a few. And when you have come in, you shall shut the door behind you and your sons; then pour it into all those vessels, and set aside the full ones."

So she went from him and shut the door behind her and her sons, who brought the vessels to her; and she poured it out. Now it came to pass, when the vessels were full, that she said to her son, "Bring me another vessel."

And he said to her, "There is not another vessel." So the oil ceased. Then she came and told the man of God. And

> *he said, "Go, sell the oil and pay your debt; and you and*
> *your sons live on the rest."*

II Kings 4:1-7

****

Story #2: The Widow of Nain

> *Now it happened, the day after, that He went into a city*
> *called Nain; and many of His disciples went with Him,*
> *and a large crowd. And when He came near the gate*
> *of the city, behold, a dead man was being carried out,*
> *the only son of his mother; and she was a widow. And a*
> *large crowd from the city was with her.*
>
> *When the Lord saw her, He had compassion on her and*
> *said to her, "Do not weep."*
>
> *Then He came and touched the open coffin, and those*
> *who carried him stood still. And He said, "Young man, I*
> *say to you, arise."*
>
> *So he who was dead sat up and began to speak. And He*
> *presented him to his mother.*

Luke 7:11-17

****

Today, many widows are highly educated, gainfully employed, and self-sufficient; however, for many others, our economy dictates the necessity of two incomes to afford to maintain comfortable lifestyles.

Paying the bills had been James's job. Now keeping them paid is mine. Yikes! Life was comfortable while my husband covered us. Thankfully, I knew how to pay bills and budget, but not having to do it was a distinct blessing.

God's word speaks to every situation we can ever face, so if the bills threaten to bring you to a worry point from time to time, meditate upon Jesus' words:

> *Therefore I say to you, do not worry about your life, what*
> *you will eat or what you will drink; nor about your body,*

154

what you will put on. Is not life more than food and the body more than clothing? Look at the birds of the air, for they neither sow nor reap nor gather into barns; yet your heavenly Father feeds them. Are you not of more value than they?

Matthew 6:25-26

————— ✍ —————

Journal your reaction to the above passages as they relate to your possible day-to-day worries.

Week Twelve: Day Three

Trust me: I am not glibly telling you not to worry and celebrate today just because that sounds like good, easy advice. I've caught myself being anxious—worrying about whether or not the money will stretch. However, I'm determined to trust God and believe His word.

Hebrews 11:1 is clear:

> *Now faith is the substance of things hoped for, the evidence of things not seen." If we could take care of everything on our own, we would have no need for God. He does His best work with that which we cannot figure out. And I believe He does miracles with a twinkle in His eye! King David wrote that throughout his whole life, he had "not seen the righteous forsaken, nor his [God's] descendants begging bread"*

So take the advice of Philippians 4:6-7 to heart:

> *Be anxious for nothing, but in everything by prayer and supplication, with thanksgiving, let your requests be made known to God; and the peace of God, which surpasses all understanding, will guard your hearts and minds through Christ Jesus.*

Journal a prayer to God discussing with Him your concerns about God meeting your needs. Be specific.

Week Thirteen

Day One
The Remodel and the Joy

It's 2024—a leap year. That means we get an extra day to honor God and become more like Christ. The year 2023 was the hardest one I've ever lived, but neither God nor my friends and family left me all alone. I'm grateful. What an example to take into the future.

Life will be different—I guess you could say it's been remodeled. So, the remodeling of my home is symbolic of my losing the physical presence of my Honey, but not the strength of the legacy of our love and marriage. The old look may be changed, but the bones are sturdy—just like the foundation of what James and I had together can never be erased. The strength of James's physical presence may be gone, but the strength he left inside of me will live on forever. The planet is better because he had been here.

****

Although your husband has passed away, use his legacy and your memories as building blocks instead of letting those blocks bury you. Continuing to live life with joy does not mean you cared for your loved one any less. You are merely allowing God to continue to use you. "The joy of the Lord is your strength" (Nehemiah 8:10). "Joy" is my word for the year!

Journal: It doesn't have to be a new year for you to choose a word on which you will focus as you make a new start. Choose an inspirational word that's used in the Bible that will center you for the next few months or a year. Journal why you are choosing this word. (Sample words: joy, hope, love, contentment, faith, grace, etc.)

Week Thirteen: Day Two

As I mentioned on day one above, during the first year after James died, I had half of my home remodeled. I lived in the other half of the house without a working kitchen while the construction was going on. Huge, heavy plastic curtains hung in several strategic spots to shield me from the dust. My spare bedroom became my makeshift kitchen as I used electric appliances—the toaster, crock pot, microwave, and air fryer—set up on a card table to prepare my meals.

The remodeling process and the subsequent new look somehow helped me weather the grief. The house was torn up for a while, but so was my life. However, I trusted Ecostar, my wonderful construction company, who had a track record and showed me evidence of having everything under control. Progress was made daily as the craftsmen labored in their specialties, and the managers double and triple checked to be sure the work was perfect. (See glossary for link to Sharon's Complete Kitchen Remodel video.)

Throughout the process, I could see God remodeling my life. James had been torn away, and the house of my emotional life was in shambles. Still, the plastic sheets of prayer kept the "dust" of despair and destructive thoughts from settling into my vital organs of trust, faith, and optimism. The Trinity was working to rebuild me as, like with my temporary galley, I learned to get things done in different ways.

When I chose "joy" to be my word for the new year, I knew the phrase "the joy of the Lord is your strength." Upon writing this section of this book, I looked up the Scripture to be sure I had the right reference. Lo and behold, the phrase I knew was the tail end of the full verse. The rest of the verse is so appropriate for our discussion that I had to include it here. It says:

Then he said to them, "Go your way, eat the fat, drink the sweet, and send portions to those for whom nothing is prepared; for this day is holy to our Lord. Do not sorrow, for the joy of the Lord is your strength"

Nehemiah 8:10

****

Yes, the time has come to allow God to remodel your understanding of yourself as a widow. You can still remember and honor your late hubby, but go ahead and start to live again. The Message Bible version says, "Go home and prepare a feast, holiday food and drink; and share it with those who don't have anything: This day is holy to God. Don't feel bad. The joy of God is your strength!" Prepare, share, and don't feel bad. Remodel!

Journal your reaction to the above Scripture as it relates to some things you can do differently as your life is remodeled.

Week Thirteen: Day Three

None of us know the turns our lives will take. I can tell you, though, without a shadow of a doubt, that change is a sure thing that will happen in your life. John F. Kenney once said, "Change is the law of life, and those who look only to the past and present are certain to miss the future."

Don't miss the future because you're paralyzed by the death of your husband and your current situation. Your existence as a widow is not a waste or a mistake.

Journal a prayer to God and talk with Him about remodeling your life. Where can you find joy?

Week Fourteen

Day One
More Smiles Than Tears

Today, January 16th, marked 8 months since I last held his warm hand. Looking back brings more smiles and sweet memories than tears these days. I went through pictures: our first formal portrait after we got married, our trip to Niagara Falls (which started our summer odysseys to follow the Underground Railroad), and our trek to Washington D.C. when we attended Obama's first inauguration. I looked at photos of events we attended with our pastor like the one taken at the California State Baptist Convention when our pastor was voted in as President. The final picture over which I lingered was taken on our last cruise along the California coast.

We traveled to many great places together. Although James has traveled ahead this time, he did not travel alone. I was a great companion, but he's spending time with a much better partner, so how can I be sad? Tears occasionally ambush me, I let them flow, then I pick up where I left off.

I'm realizing that the rhythm of life does indeed smooth out and start again. God heals broken hearts.

Journal: What are your favorite photos of your husband and yourself? Describe them here and remind yourself of why you like these pictures so much.

Week Fourteen: Day Two

Cameras didn't exist in Jesus' day. In order to have a portrait, one would have to sit still for hours as a painter captured your image on his canvas. Perhaps that's why the Mona Lisa is not smiling; she just simply got tired of posing. And it's ridiculous to think all thirteen men in attendance at the Last Supper all sat along one side of the table. Still, I feel the artist got the expressions right with no one smiling at the moment Jesus announced, "One of you will betray me."

Today, as I scroll through the 12,013 photos and 1,174 videos on my phone, few pictures of people have been captured without smiles. What a lovely reminder of how life has been and of how it can be again—if I allow it. What a hoot to be able to look back at captured time when smiles were on each face.

Let's look forward today about a face we shall all see one day if we have placed our hope in Christ. Revelation 22:3-5 will put a smile on every believer's face:

> *And there shall be no more curse, but the throne of God and of the Lamb shall be in it, and His servants shall serve Him. They shall see His face, and His name shall be on their foreheads. There shall be no night there: They need no lamp nor light of the sun, for the Lord God gives them light. And they shall reign forever and ever.*

****

Come on. No more curse.

No more night.

No need for lamps or light from the sun.

Light coming from the Lord God Himself.

Protection because of being marked with God's name.

Seeing God on His throne.

Seeing Jesus, the Lamb of God, sitting right there with God.

Being one of, and in the presence of, God's servants, all functioning in service to Him on one accord.

You must be smiling by now.

Journal: With the above passage in mind, and excluding the pictures of your husband that you discussed in the journal of Day 1 of this week, what are some things about the Lord, your life now, and your future that make you smile?

Week Fourteen: Day Three

I believe Jesus smiled at times during His ministry. He must have smiled to see the gratitude from those He healed. I think He smiled when he dealt with children—He drew them to Himself as He explained how to have simple faith.

> *Then they brought little children to Him, that He might touch them; but the disciples rebuked those who brought them. But when Jesus saw it, He was greatly displeased and said to them, "Let the little children come to Me, and do not forbid them; for of such is the kingdom of God. Assuredly, I say to you, whoever does not receive the kingdom of God as a little child will by no means enter it.*

> Mark 10:13-15

Journal: Ask God about what makes Him smile. Through your pen, talk with Him here about getting your genuine smile back. Discuss who He wants to reach through your smile.

Week Fifteen

Day One
Return from Visiting Grief

It's been 9 months since James Elliott (otherwise affectionately known by others as Daddy, Pop, Deacon Elliott, friend, and "Honey" to me) moved from Earth to Glory. Nine months is significant as that is enough time for a new human being to be completely developed and born. It's also the mother's relief to be finished with the weight of the pregnancy. She can look back on that time and seeing what beauty has come of it, she can live joyfully in her new role. In much the same way, once we leave the places we visit, we take the pictures and the memories with us to look back on with gratitude and smile for having had such a wonderfully good and blessed time.

I've learned that like the necessity of pregnancy if you want new life, and the necessity of vacations for energy boosts to keep moving forward, grief is a place we will all most likely visit one day, but we're not supposed to make it a permanent residence. The 21 years represented by all the pictures I took—from the first time I laid eyes on James, to our last picture together, to the last time we held hands—represent the wonderful memories I will always cherish. I choose to return from visiting grief and step back into life.

We do not dishonor our loved ones by continuing to live. This is the joy that comes in the morning after the night of weeping.

Journal: How do you feel about letting go of grief?

Week Fifteen: Day Two

In 1946, Billy Holiday recorded the song "Good Morning Heart-ache." In it, she personifies heartache, speaking to it with resolve because it's a regular visitor in her life that just won't go away. She has accepted the fact of heartache's permanent residence in her life.

The building that is our life was not constructed to house heart-ache as a roommate. Grief has visited, but the time has come to allow it to move on.

Be careful though. Do not replace grief with guilt. Does your heart believe you are abandoning your husband if you allow yourself to be happy? Do you feel a sense of guilt if night arrives, and you realize you haven't thought about him all day? It is quite all right to allow yourself to think on other things and other people besides your late husband. It is also quite all right to continue to think about him in healthy ways. Tears have a timetable all their own. Time and time again, I keep hearing, "Everyone grieves in her own way." Your sensitive feelings are not being downgraded nor disregarded. I am just encouraging you to allow the Spirit of God to begin to heal your heart.

When we speak of moving on from grief, Psalm 30:5b is usually the verse we hear being quoted. "Weeping may endure for a night, but joy comes in the morning." The question remains, "How do I get through that night?" Our answer lies in another famously quoted psalm.

The 23rd Psalm is a soft pillow of comfort. Read it through 3 times before moving on through this day's reflective time:

> *The Lord is my shepherd; I shall not want [I have everything I need].*
>
> *He makes me to lie down in green pastures; He leads me beside the still waters.*
>
> *He restores my soul; He leads me in the paths of righteousness for His name's sake.*

Yea, though I walk through the valley of the shadow of death, *I will fear no evil; for You are with me; your rod and Your staff, they comfort me.*

You prepare a table before me in the presence of my enemies; You anoint my head with oil; my cup runs over.

Surely goodness and mercy shall follow me all the days of my life; and I will dwell in the house of the Lord forever.

(Brackets and bold italics added)

****

Full books have been written seeking to unpack the richness of each phrase of this beautiful Psalm, so I won't try to go into all of its wonders here. I will, however, point your attention to how it relates to our current discussion. Since the Lord is our shepherd, part of the "everything I need" includes Him being our personal escort through grief, i.e. "the valley of the shadow of death." As we walk together, His presence both dispels fear and provides comfort. Notice, though, that life doesn't end just on the other side of grief. The Lord goes on with us to lift us to new heights by handling our enemies, anointing our heads, and providing abundantly. As we move forward, goodness and mercy are our rear guard as we realize our forever dwelling place is not only our heavenly home, but God's continual presence.

Journal: As you reflect on Psalm 23 and Psalm 30:5, journal your reactions as they relate to moving on from grief.

Week Fifteen: Day Three

Journal: Go to God in prayer about evicting grief, especially its crippling elements.

Week Sixteen

Day One
Snatching Back my Power

It's now been 10 months since my amazing husband, James Elliott, moved from this life into the next. Grief is changing. It is weakening as I realize it is drawing its power from me. At first, it seemed like a formidable, tear-producing monster, gripping me with vice-like strength. But as time moves on and I find that God has things He wants me to do, I've begun to busy my hands with those things. Lo and behold, I've discovered grief was not gripping me, I was gripping it. I was giving it its power by holding it so close. As I became willing to let it go, it began to starve.

Now, grief was not happy to be weaned away from its source. It yelled at me, sometimes through the disapproving looks and comments of others who questioned my true love for James.

"If you really loved your husband, you wouldn't be thinking about moving on."

"You're dishonoring your husband by taking so many of his pictures down."

"You're insensitive for giving his clothes away."

"It's too soon. You're not ready to explore a new relationship."

All lies. Continuing to live and feel happiness are not signs of disrespect for the relationship you had with your husband. Grief tries its best to keep us from the truth. Our hands cannot be so full of grief that we have no capacity to grasp God's new plans. Academy Award winning actress, director, and producer Regina King became acquainted with grief all too personally when her 26-year-old son Ian died by suicide. Ms. King has said, "Grief is love with no place to go."

As we allow our love to be released for those living who still need it, we find our love for our late loved one does not diminish at all. In fact, love deepens and widens because we have been empowered by the love of the one we once held close.

For months, I still wore my wedding ring, but I wore it on my right hand—the hand that represents power. And I needed that power because I did not expect to be at that point in my life traveling alone, sleeping alone, and having new experiences with no one close to share them with. I miss hugging, kissing, and having someone who would look at me in a crowded room like I was the only other person on the planet. All of that being gone really stinks. However, I am hearing God clearly every time I open the Word, praying more deeply, and caring even more intimately for my business associates, family members, and friends.

I still cry about missing James sometimes, but I smile a whole lot more. God is good and He is still in control.

Journal: How can you begin to take back the power grief has stolen from your life?

Week Sixteen: Day Two

One of my previous books, *A Woman God Can Bless*, is an in-depth study of Ephesians 4:17-32. This passage gives us a clear understanding of what we should put off and put on. In other words, in terms of Christian character traits, what does God intend for us to let go of, and what does He intend for us to pick up. Chapter 1 explains that "this book will help us look at our lifestyle, our choices, our habits, and our beliefs, etc., to be sure we are doing our part and are on the right track. Sometimes we get so caught up in the day-to-day vicissitudes of life that we become slipshod in what we would consider to be small details; thus, we place ourselves in a position in which we cannot receive God's blessings." (*A Woman God Can Bless*, Iron Stream Media/Harambee Press, 2020)

So, for our present reflection about grief, let's glean from Ephesians 4:17-32:

> *This I say, therefore, and testify in the Lord, that you should no longer walk as the rest of the Gentiles walk, in the futility of their mind, having their understanding darkened, being alienated from the life of God, because of the ignorance that is in them, because of the blindness of their heart; who, being past feeling, have given themselves over to lewdness, to work all uncleanness with greediness. But you have not so learned Christ, if indeed you have heard Him and have been taught by Him, as the truth is in Jesus: that you put off,* concerning your former conduct, *the old man which grows corrupt according to the deceitful lusts, and be renewed in the spirit of your mind, and that you put on the new man which was created according to God, in true righteousness and holiness.*
>
> *Therefore, putting away lying, "Let each one of you speak truth with his neighbor," for we are members of one another. "Be angry, and do not sin": do not let the sun*

go down on your wrath, nor give place to the devil. Let him who stole steal no longer, but rather let him labor, working with his hands what is good, that he may have something to give him who has need. Let no corrupt word proceed out of your mouth, but what is good for necessary edification, that it may impart grace to the hearers. And do not grieve the Holy Spirit of God, by whom you were sealed for the day of redemption. Let all bitterness, wrath, anger, clamor, and evil speaking be put away from you, with all malice. And be kind to one another, tenderhearted, forgiving one another, even as God in Christ forgave you.

Ephesians 4:17-32
(Bold italics added)

****

By now in your grief journey, you have possibly ascribed to the idea that operating as a widow with an ever-present grief mindset is your "new normal." I understand that mindset, but I also understand that allowing myself to be settled with grief gives grief permission to weigh me down and keep me from soaring again. I have lived through sitting in the widow's seat smack dab in front of my husband's casket as final words are said over him. I have lived through the parting view when my eyes were so full of tears that I couldn't see his face. I have lived through watching his coffin being sealed into the crypt behind that heavy piece of marble. I have lived through making all the final contacts as I executed our trust.

Our new normal, yours as well as mine, is the power we've amassed because of what we have lived through. Now we can put off that former conduct and emerge renewed in the spirit of our minds, putting off bitterness and putting on joy. We're leaving behind the bleakness of winter and stepping into the fresh air of a new spring morning.

Journal your reaction to the above passage as it relates to anything you're now spiritually, emotionally, and psychologically putting off and putting on.

Week Sixteen: Day Three

Snatching back our power only works to our advantage when we do so by God's leading. In every area of life, we are to present our whole selves to God as His living sacrifices. Paul puts this idea succinctly in Romans 12:1-2 when he writes:

> *I beseech you therefore, brethren, by the mercies of God,*
> *that you present your bodies a living sacrifice, holy,*
> *acceptable to God, which is your reasonable service. And*
> *do not be conformed to this world, but be transformed by*
> *the renewing of your mind, that you may prove what is*
> *that good and acceptable and perfect will of God.*
>
> Romans 12:1-2

Journal a prayer to God in which you present yourself to Him as a living sacrifice. Honestly talk with Him about any misgivings you may have about this. Do you still trust His goodness? With no misgivings, do you still believe in His power? Are you confident in God's ability to protect your heart? If you do all this putting off and putting on, can you count on God not to let you down?

Week Seventeen

Day One
Tired of Grief, Moving Forward

It's April 16th and today marks 11 months since James left. Frankly, I'm tired of him being dead now. I'm tired of waking up without him, going to sleep without him, and watching TV without him. I cook for myself and always have too much food left over that I get tired of eating so it goes bad, and I have to throw it out. I come into a dark house unless I've remembered to leave a light on all day if I had to leave.

This past month held some special reminders that James wasn't here.

The car battery died so I had to maneuver through calling AAA, talking with the driver about whatever the problem was, taking the car to the dealership for a new battery which was a "special" battery (of course) because it had to be hooked up to the dealer's computer to sync all the bells and whistles. James would have handled that.

A health problem popped up related to one of my medications. I had to run around to various pharmacies, make multiple calls to my doctor, and wait on hold with my insurance company to get things straightened out. This took several days while I was going without my medication. There was no one here to talk or complain to about this, or to help me through the concern. James would have been here for that.

My wall heater in my house was on the fritz. It went out while it had been really cold outside, so it was also cold inside. To heat the house, I had to use electric space heaters, thus running up the electric bill. James would have been taking care of that.

I empty all the little trash cans in the house into the large, smelly trash cans in the yard. Then, every Sunday night, I take the nasty trash cans to the front curb, and every Monday afternoon, I pull those huge, rolling monstrosities back up the driveway and into their space in the yard. For the past two weeks, it has been raining on Sunday. James used to tangle with those city trash receptacles.

I'm keeping up with the bills. James did that.

I'm figuring out who will take me and pick me up from the airport when I travel. James was my personal Uber--and his service included a hug and a kiss at drop off and pick up. No extra charge!

There's no one special to call when I'm out of town in hotel rooms alone. There's no one special to say, "Did I tell you 'I love you today'?" There's no one wondering why I didn't call when I'm later than usual getting home. There are no winks, loving looks, or hugs. There are no kisses.

I am no one's "person."

I'm tired of James being gone.

Of course, I know I have to be a realist in this real world. I know all the things that have been said to me:

God is with you. He's now your husband.

You'll get through this.

You're strong.

This season will pass.

So please, don't say any of it; just understand.

I'm more than thankful for God, for Jesus, for Holy Spirit. and for you. You've been praying for me, and I can tell. Please keep it up.

Journal: What are the insensitive things people have said or done? Did you handle their words or actions well? Have you forgiven them? What are you tired of? How has your grief made you stronger? How do you see life differently?

Week Seventeen: Day Two

Isn't it frustrating to want something you just cannot have? I cannot have James back, but I realize I really enjoyed being a wife in a relationship, so I opened my mind and heart to the possibility of a new personal connection. Well, in case you haven't noticed, we're living in a new dating era. Today, people meet via the internet more than any other way.

I started being catfished. That's when men put fake photos and biographies on the internet in an effort to lure you into dating relationships often with the goal in mind to trick you out of money. Apparently, some men feel like widows are easy prey because their loneliness and grief cause them to reach out naively for companionship.

Not all internet relationship sites are corrupt, so I'm not speaking against all legitimate dating services. I met James through a dating service, but back several decades ago, the interested parties had to physically go to the dating service's office to be interviewed. This way, women knew someone besides ourselves had laid actual eyes on the man, and questions could be asked of the workers regarding those in whom we were interested.

Nowadays, be very careful because even legitimate dating services cannot screen out liars. You have to be watchful and smart. Never give your home address. Never send the man money. Never meet him alone the first few times. In fact, if your conversation goes as far as arousing a desire to meet in person, I suggest you do so in public places and perhaps meet with another couple who you know.

In First Timothy, Paul gives the young pastor advice about how to work with widows in the church. The Message Bible version paraphrases 1 Timothy 5:8-15 in this way:

> *Take care of widows who are destitute. If a widow has*
> *family members to take care of her, let them learn that*
> *religion begins at their own doorstep and that they*

should pay back with gratitude some of what they have received. This pleases God immensely.

You can tell a legitimate widow by the way she has put all her hope in God, praying to him constantly for the needs of others as well as her own. But a widow who exploits people's emotions and pocketbooks—well, there's nothing to her. Tell these things to the people so that they will do the right thing in their extended family. Anyone who neglects to care for family members in need repudiates the faith. That's worse than refusing to believe in the first place.

Sign some widows up for the special ministry of offering assistance. They will in turn receive support from the church. They must be over sixty, married only once, and have a reputation for helping out with children, strangers, tired Christians, the hurt and troubled.

Don't put young widows on this list. No sooner will they get on than they'll want to get off, obsessed with wanting to get a husband rather than serving Christ in this way. By breaking their word, they're liable to go from bad to worse, frittering away their days on empty talk, gossip, and trivialities. No, I'd rather the young widows go ahead and get married in the first place, have children, manage their homes, and not give critics any foothold for finding fault. Some of them have already left and gone after Satan.

1 Timothy 5:8-15

****

Lots of churches don't have widows' ministries like this early church must have had. However, the spirit of the passage is clear in three areas. First, a widow's extended family should be actively involved in taking care of her physical needs when she requires assistance.

Second, whether there's a special auxiliary in a particular congregation or not, widows have a place of service—ministry opportunities—in the church. This includes the many different ways widows can be involved with "helping out with children, strangers, tired Christians, the hurt and troubled."

Third, widows who want to be married can go ahead and do so rather than "frittering away their days on empty talk, gossip, and trivialities."

Journal your reaction to the above passage as it relates to your thoughts about remaining single, starting to date again, and/or remarriage.

Week Seventeen: Day Three

Even though there are both positives and negatives to living alone or launching into a new romantic relationship, Psalm 37:4 is still true.

Delight yourself also in the Lord, and He shall give you the desires of your heart.

Journal: Talk with God in prayer here about your thoughts and feelings regarding having or not having a new romantic relationship. How is your heart being led?

Week Eighteen

Day One
The Wonderful Thing About Love

One year ago today, I was watching a miracle that changed my life. My husband, James D. Elliott, took flight to Glory. I held onto his arm until the two kind young people driving the mortuary van pulled away from the curb with him. After returning to the room he just left, I broke down. I don't know how long I cried.

The next week-and-a-half rushed by with notifications, mortuary planning meetings, calls to the cemetery, and the like. Friends visited regularly as did the tears. The wake, the memorial service, the burial, and the repass were all well-attended and comforting.

All too soon, although friends continued to pray for me, everyone went back to their lives, and I started my new one--alone. Sure, church friends, family members, personal buddies, and business associates were still around, but I came home to an empty house. I cried a lot.

But you know what, God's word is true. "Weeping may endure for a night, but joy comes in the morning." Each day actually got a little easier and a little brighter. On the rare moments when I cried, the Holy Spirit reminded me, "You know you're crying for yourself, don't you?" When I protested my need to do so because I was all alone, He countered, "You know you have Me, don't you?"

My heart needed to let go of James's ability to fill the aloneness in my world. The memories had to be fully understood for what they are--lovely reflections of the past. Trusting God for today and tomorrow no longer included James. No one can be him. No one can be like him. No one on the planet will ever love me like James loved me. I will never love another man like I loved James.

But the wonderful thing about love is that we can show love to others and be loved by others uniquely. Love is just that wonderful. After all, "God is love." As I continue to grow to be more and more like Him, I'm hopeful there may be another special man-of-God in my life. When and if God sends another love my way, that relationship won't be a denial of the one I had with James. It will be another affirmation of God's continued love for me.

Don't be afraid to let God love you.

Journal: What is happening in your life through which you are feeling God's love?

Week Eighteen: Day Two

Ecclesiastes 12:13 communicates a very important truth about all of mankind. Solomon writes, "Let us hear the conclusion of the whole matter: Fear God and keep His commandments, for this is man's all." Several other Bible translations say that fearing God and keeping His commandments is "the whole duty of man." So, whether we are well or ill; young or old; educated or uneducated; rich or poor; widows, wives, or single; the central goal of our lives is to bring glory to God.

And how do we show that we are fearing God and keeping His commandments? That's easy: through our imitation of the character of God exercised through our love for others. John, the disciple who nicknamed himself as "the disciple whom Jesus loved" would obviously know all about the connection between God, love, and us. (See John 13:23, 19:26, 20:2, 21:7, and 21:20.) He explains:

> *Beloved, let us love one another, for love is of God; and everyone who loves is born of God and knows God. He who does not love does not know God, for God is love. In this the love of God was manifested toward us, that God has sent His only begotten Son into the world, that we might live through Him. In this is love, not that we loved God, but that He loved us and sent His Son to be the propitiation for our sins. Beloved, if God so loved us, we also ought to love one another...*
>
> *Love has been perfected among us in this: that we may have boldness in the day of judgment; because as He is, so are we in this world. There is no fear in love; but perfect love casts out fear, because fear involves torment. But he who fears has not been made perfect in love. We love Him because He first loved us.*
>
> I John 4:7-11 and 17-19

Journal your reaction to the above passages as they relate to how you are showing love to others.

Week Eighteen: Day Three

We have weathered quite an ordeal in the passing of our husbands. Although each man was unique, each relationship unparalleled, and each death unforgettable, the unifying factor between us ladies is that we, their widows, are here without them. The passing of our loved one is why we've gathered around this book, but love is also the absolute best remedy for every aspect of grief. I'm confident that God will restore your joy, your smile, your confidence, and your trust in the beauty of the world He created for you to enjoy even as you live in it "after him."

Journal a prayer to God expressing your love for Him and accepting His unparalleled love for you.

Epilogue

On week 2, I made you a promise with these words:

On the day James died, I wrote a post that included these sentences: "Always taking care of business! We all saw how he lived. One day, I'll tell you the story of how he was a shining example of how to die."

Well, today's the day to fulfill that promise to you…

Two nights before his birthday, James poked his head in my office and was holding his side. He said, "I think you need to take me to the hospital. This pain is pretty bad."

"Okay, let's go." I popped up out of my desk chair, threw on my shoes and a coat, and off we went. The emergency room doctor suggested he be given pain meds because he was probably experiencing pain from gall stones.

"Think again," was my response. "Let's do what has to be done to find out the true cause of the pain instead of guessing and throwing pills at the effect.

The doctor relented. "Well, I suppose we could admit him and do some further tests."

"Let's try that." I looked at James and knew he was glad to have someone there advocating for him.

The next day, the diagnosis was returned: stage 4 liver cancer. James faced the diagnosis head on. Since it was 2 days before Christmas, he had to wait a few weeks to go to Torrance Memorial Cancer Care Center to meet with the specialist. At the first meeting, James basically told the doctor, "Give it to me straight." He had already decided to give whatever treatments they suggested one shot. That's what his dad had done.

To make a long story short, none of the treatments worked, but he devotedly followed every doctor's order. Above the medical side of the five months from his diagnosis to his death, his interpersonal and spiritual side shone.

First, he clung to his belief in God's ability to heal him. After he died, I found a prayer he had been praying in his quiet times with the Lord. Only once had he allowed his mouth to say to his son, "I'm dying." The rest of his comments about his illness were confessions of faith in his victory over it.

Second, James called anyone with whom he'd had cross words and peacefully settled each score. There weren't lots of people, but he reached out to apologize and get relationships straight just in case he would soon be facing his Maker. Saying, "I'm sorry, I was wrong," were not phrases his pride easily let him enunciate, so this took the humility of a soul wanting to ultimately please God with his life.

Third, James spent time talking with those he loved. He allowed his niece to make a video of him as she asked him questions about his life. He made phone calls and accepted visits from friends and family members. Even as he weakened, he let each person know that he knew who they were and why they were special to him. After it was too hard to speak, his eyes still knowingly locked on his visitors so they went away feeling loved and acknowledged.

Fourth, although it took some time, once he could no longer care for his own physical needs, he graciously realized it was our honor to do all we could do to care for him. He still tried helping us to help him. Once he suggested we line the hallway with plastic just in case he couldn't quite make it from the bedroom to the bathroom. This suggestion came after he could no longer get around without his wheelchair. He also came up with the idea of using one of his neckties to help us turn him onto his side. We were to loop the necktie to a bar outside of his window. Then when he needed to turn onto his side, he could help us by pulling himself over. The problem with that plan was that the window would have to remain open, and he was cold most of the time. Because he had lost so much weight, we could turn him without his help, but he was still trying to do what he always did—handle things.

Finally, all the way until the day he died, he took care of me. He once heard people in the living room challenging me with their judgement of something I had done. As I attempted to explain in contradiction to their viewpoint, James rang his bell. (His kids had given him a bell he could use to summon help if ever he was alone in the room. Oh, to hear that bell today!) I jumped up to go see about him. He didn't have any needs; he was just rescuing me from the assault.

Until he could no longer talk, he told everyone over and over again how much he loved me and couldn't imagine going through this ordeal without me. He consistently encouraged me, built me up, and wanted me to be with him whenever he was awake. Even his son commented, "You just want your baby to be near."

One afternoon, after caring for his needs, as I was rearranging his bedding, I caught him watching me. He said, "You're tired." His tone wasn't belittling, accusatory, or sorrowful; it was just matter-of-fact. In those two tiny words, he was conveying the fact that he still saw me— he still understood me. I responded, "Yes, Honey, but I've got you."

Those were the last words he was ever able to speak to me. In that revelation, both he and I knew that in a very real sense, he'd be continuing to take care of me by going Home to Jesus. God knew how long I'd be able to keep up the pace of James's care, but I was doggedly determined to be his primary caregiver. And James knew I'd keep doing the job, no matter what. Although neither of us wanted it to be so, he knew if he let his cancer-ridden body go, he could rest, and I could rest.

All the legal paperwork was in order, all the bills were figured out, all the final arrangements were written, and everyone who knew him clearly understood he loved us. His life had been lived and his salvation was settled.

Now that's the way to die.

Sharon's Memories

(This is the eulogy Sharon delivered at James's homegoing service.)

James and I decided to walk through this cancer journey by faith. We took Psalm 103:1-5 as being literally for us.

> *¹Bless the Lord, O my soul;*
>
> *And all that is within me, bless His holy name! [Keep speaking well of God]*
>
> *²Bless the Lord, O my soul,*
>
> *And forget not all His benefits: [Keep counting our blessings]*
>
> *³Who forgives all your iniquities,*
>
> *Who heals all your diseases, [Cancer is a disease God can heal]*
>
> *⁴Who redeems your life from destruction, [Cancer was being destructive]*
>
> *Who crowns you with lovingkindness and tender mercies, [no matter what, God loved us and was extending His mercy toward us; James went through this ordeal without pain]*

5Who satisfies your mouth with good things, [we leaned on this one when he started to lose his appetite]

So that your youth is renewed like the eagle's. [overall, he was healthy in his youth, so we needed his youth to be renewed]

I then posted these verses on index cards and taped them up around the house.

We also decided to act as if these verses were really true for us. We made plans for our lives to go on as usual because God was about to work a miracle in James's body.

To believe God and then act otherwise is to deify the natural over the spiritual. Either believe wholeheartedly or don't believe at all. Not until God clearly shows us He's going in another direction do we get to leave space for an exception. Faith was the substance of our hope for James's healing. Faith was the evidence of the healing we did not yet see. We figured God wanted us to continue seeing doctors so the doctors could see the miracle.

So we started the treatment regimen. I had my calendar for everywhere we had to go and everything he had to do. Every appointment time and location was put in the book and kept because we believed God was going to use all of this as part of the testimony. Sure, God could have zapped him well at any time, but like the lepers in the Bible, we figured he'd be healed as he went along. So, we kept living life.

But James kept getting sicker.

Now this is the part where nonbelievers think they have us. They'll start saying things like:

"Prayer doesn't work."

"Praying is nothing but empty words to the air and then you Christians just flip the script when things don't work out like you "prayed."

"Your God isn't real."

Well, skeptics, you have 2 things twisted:

First, prayer is not a magic, abracadabra, hocus pocus. Prayer is a conversation with God. And even when we're asking or even begging God for something, as our omniscient, omnipotent, and loving Parent,

He still gets to decide the timing and how He will answer. God can be trusted.

Second, God is not a cosmic genie, a bellhop, or our personal servant. He is the Christian's Lord and Savior in the person of Jesus Christ and in the power of the Holy Spirit. God is sovereign. He is running the universe, not us.

So, as we were quoting Psalm 103 to Him, He began challenging us to believe all of Scripture. He pointed out that Psalm 103 wasn't the only Scripture in the Bible that applied to our situation. In our case, God started showing me Scriptures we like to skip over:

Hebrews 9:27 – It is appointed unto every person to die.

Psalm 116:15 – Precious in the sight of the Lord is the death of His saints.

Job 13:15 – Thou He slay me, yet will I trust Him.

When the Rapture happens, the many saints who have died will resurrect. That scripture cannot be true unless some saints have died.

Great multitudes around the throne cannot be true unless some saints have died.

The Bible tells us there are martyrs in heaven—that cannot be true unless some saints have died.

Unless the Rapture happens, we are all going to die and we will all face God whether you believe that to be your truth or not—it's the truth.

James was a straightforward man. He would tell it like he saw it—straight up, no chaser. He was right a lot, and contrary to popular opinion, he was wrong sometimes. I began having to prove my points by Googling the facts. Still, he was straight up. How he got away with it, I don't know, but he wore this button to work every day: "If you don't know Christ, go to Hell." That wasn't a pronouncement of a curse; it was just a fact.

James loved his children, grandchildren, great-grandchildren, extended family, and friends. Any scores God led him to settle, he reached out to make that happen. And I know without a shadow of a doubt that he loved me. I adored him. Still, most of all, he loved Jesus. He would like you to know one more time—heaven and hell are real. Thanks to Jesus in His life, his sins were forgiven and early in the morning on Tuesday, May 16, I watched his body let his spirit step peacefully into Heaven completely whole and healed.

He taught us all he could and has left us amazing memories. Let's keep our theology right, though. James is not looking down on us because He's got a much better face to look at—that of His Lord and Savior, Jesus Christ. Let it be part of his legacy that those of you who don't have a relationship with Jesus start one today.

This applies to family and friends. My husband would want you to go past honoring him and make a commitment to honor God from this day forward.

Everyone, please bow your heads:

I'm going to give you five options, and only if the statement applies to you, I'm asking you to stand and remain standing for just a moment until I can pray for you.

Option 1: If you've never seriously said "yes" to Jesus, please stand.

Option 2: If you have strayed away from Jesus, please stand.

Option 3: If you no longer think you need Jesus and you're willing to give Him another chance in your life, please stand.

Option 4: If you've been waiting for the right time to meet Jesus, this is it. Please stand.

Option 5: If you want to go to heaven (where James is), and you're willing to give this Christianity thing an honest try, I promise you that God will not disappoint you. Please stand.

Father God, in the name of Jesus, and in the power of Your Holy Spirit, come into the lives of those you see standing. Be the God they need you to be. Surround them with Your love and impact their lives so completely that they'll never turn away from You. Give them the confidence of Your presence. Thank you for drawing them to Yourself. In Jesus' mighty name, Amen.

Please be seated. Today, May 26, 2023, is the start of your new life with Jesus. Welcome to the Kingdom of God! When you get to heaven, after you've spent time gazing on the face of Jesus and taking in the glory your new digs, find James and let him know that his life and testimony were at least part of what God used to draw you to Himself.

Whether you're on Zoom or present in the building in person, thank you for being here. I appreciate every way you have poured out your love. James was my love. I called him "Honey," I'm not going to tell you his nickname for me. I miss him so much.

Notes

From Week Two, Day Three
What we have to handle when death takes our husband away.

I. Final arrangements for disposition of his body

    A. If there will be an autopsy and an investigation

    B. If there will be a funeral

        1. Decide who will be involved in making all the following decisions

        2. Choosing a mortuary

            a. Financial arrangements for the funeral

            b. Service date

                i. Funeral package

                ii. Casket

                iii. Embalming

                iv. Etc.

        3. Choosing a cemetery

    C. If there will be cremation

II. Notifications

    A. Immediate next of kin

    B. Pastor

    C. His employer

    D. Your employer

E. Other next of kin and friends

    1. Do you have the password to his phone, computer, and/ or tablet in order to get to his contacts?

III. Personal finances

A. Is everything already in your name?

B. Bank accounts and ATM cards

    1. Checking accounts – joint and personal

    2. Savings accounts – joint and personal

    3. Business accounts

C. Investments

    1. IRAs

    2. Stocks

    3. Savings bonds

    4. Etc.

D. Social Security

E. Pensions

F. Home bills

    1. Mortgage or rent

        a. Homeowners' insurance

    2. Taxes

    3. Utilities

    4. Electricity

    5. Gas

    6. Trash service

        a. Phone (home or cell – your phone and his phone

    7. Credit cards

    8. His car(s)

G. What will you do with your husband's clothes and other personal belongings? (Having a living trust softens this decision. Decide who gets what long before your husband dies.)

From Week Three, Day One

———

On the website Everplans.com, you will find a comprehensive article succinctly detailing views about cremation from different faiths and denominations. In short, cremation is acceptable in many Christian denominations. For Presbyterians, there is no clear commandment, but they generally do not support cremation. Cremation is prohibited in the Eastern Orthodox Church and in the Muslim faith. For Mormons, cremation is not prohibited but it is not encouraged. For Jewish people, views on cremation vary by degrees of orthodoxy, and in the Hindu faith, all are cremated except for babies, children, and saints.

Read the full article at:
https://www.everplans.com/articles/13-different-religious-perspectives-on-cremation

From Week Five, Day Two

For each of the characteristics in the left column, write in your plan for how you can live out that characteristic in your life.

Characteristic from Colossians 3:12-16	Plan for Building or Adding this Characteristic to My Life
Tender mercies	
Kindness	
Humility	
Meekness	
Longsuffering	
Bearing with one another	
Forgiving one another	
Love	
The peace of God	
Thankfulness	
Let the Word of Christ dwell inside richly in all wisdom	
Teaching and admonishing one another in psalms and hymns and spiritual songs	
Singing with grace in your hearts to the Lord	

From Week Eight, Day Two

———

Explanation of the Rapture from The Billy Graham Evangelistic Association:
        https://billygraham.org/answer/what-is-the-rapture/

****

From Week Thirteen, Day Two

———

Sharon's Complete Kitchen Renovation Story:
        https://www.youtube.com/watch?v=_IYfTVrrIQ8

www.ingramcontent.com/pod-product-compliance
Lightning Source LLC
Chambersburg PA
CBHW020228130626
46549CB00005B/1795